Producer & International Distributor
eBookPro Publishing
www.ebook-pro.com

Pumpkin Carving Stencils for Halloween
Made Easy Press

Contact: agency@ebook-pro.com

ISBN **9789655753745**

How to Carve Your Pumpkin

Using the 50+ stencils in this book, you can carve the spookiest, cutest, most impressive pumpkin this Halloween in just a few simple steps!

Start by putting together the tools and equipment you will need:

- A pumpkin
- A sharp knife
- An ice cream scoop or big spoon
- A paring knife
- Scissors
- Tape
- A sharp pencil, needle, pins, or a fork

Step 1
Choose a pumpkin that is nice and round, with a flat base. Make sure it is firm and around the size you want, and that the stem is green and intact.

Step 2
Set up outside, or somewhere you can make a mess. Cut a circle out of the top or back of the pumpkin, just big enough to fit your hand through.

Step 3
Using the ice cream scoop or spoon, scoop out the pulp and seeds until the inside of your pumpkin is smooth and clean.

Step 4
Pick your desired stencil and cut out the page along the scissors mark. Tape the page onto the front of your pumpkin. You might need to make small cuts in the sides so that it lays flat. Don't worry if it isn't perfect!

Step 5
Use the pencil, needle, pins, or fork to poke holes into the pumpkin around the border of the black part of the design. Make sure the holes are close together, no more than half an inch apart.

Step 6
Remove the tape and the stencil. You should see all the holes you poked forming the outline of your shape. Now, take the paring knife and carve along the design, using the holes as a guide. Push the pieces out and watch your design come to life.

Step 7
Insert a candle, LED light, or some string lights into your carved pumpkin to give it an extra-special Halloween effect!
Happy holidays!

Pumpkin Carving Stencils for Halloween

50+ Easy Spooky, Creepy, Scary, Funny Templates for Crafting the Perfect Fall Decoration with Your Kids, Teens, Family, and Friends

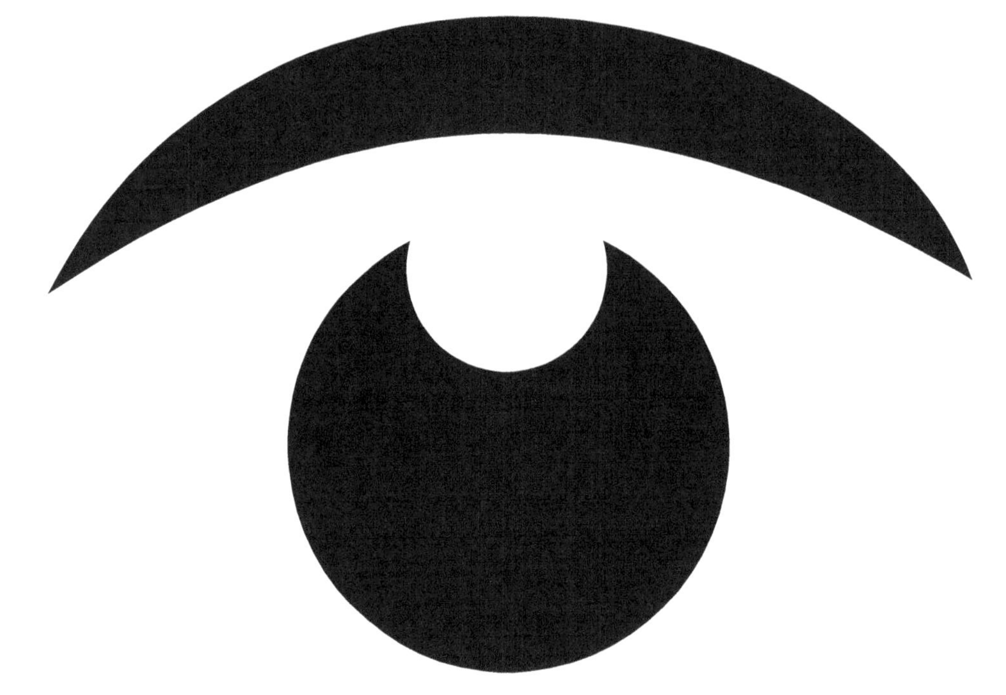

Thank you so much for reading
Pumpkin Carving Stencils for Halloween
I hope you...

We'd appreciate it so much if you would consider going to Amazon
and leaving a review.
Your reviews help us bring you more fun, family-friendly content like
this book.

About Made Easy Press

At Made Easy Press, our goal is to bring you beautifully designed,
thoughtful gifts and products.

We strive to make complicated things – easy. Whether it's learning new
skills or putting memories into words, our books are led by values of
family, creativity, and self-care and we take joy in creating authentic
experiences that make people truly happy.

Look out for other books by Made Easy Press here!